The Complete Guide to Soft Diet

Easy and Quick Recipes

Jacqueline S. Perkins

Contents

Chapter One

Introduction

Introduction

Foods that are easy to digest make up a soft food diet, also known as a bland diet. They have a soft texture and a low fiber content. Eat foods that are easy to swallow and don't require much chewing. Spicy, fried, or gassy foods should be avoided.

Soft foods in small pieces that don't require much chewing make up a soft diet. This lowers your risk of choking and eases chewing and swallowing pain. A soft diet is frequently a transitional diet or a return to normal eating, but it can also be a permanent lifestyle change in some cases.

Foods that are easy to chew and digest are included in a soft diet. Soft diets, which consist of soft and easy-to-digest foods, are frequently used in clinical settings. People who have trouble swallowing, those who have had abdominal surgery, and those who have other medical problems are frequently prescribed them. Foods that are soft and easy to chew and swallow are included in a soft diet.

Chopped, ground, mashed, pureed, or moist foods are all acceptable. If you've had surgery on your head, neck, or stomach, you might need to stick to this diet. If you have problems chewing or swallowing food, you may need to follow this diet. Your dietitian will explain how to stick to this diet and what liquid consistency you should drink.

After a long day in the dentist's chair, a hearty meal may tempt you, but your dentist or oral surgeon may advise you to eat only soft foods following certain dental procedures, such as extractions and implants, to avoid damage to your teeth, gums, crowns, or other prosthetic work. Learn why eating soft foods after some dental procedures is necessary, as well as some great options for a soft food diet, so you're prepared for your procedure.

Doctors usually recommend a soft food diet when patients have trouble swallowing due to mouth or jaw injuries or gastrointestinal problems. It does not have to be boring because the diet is much more than jelly and soup.

Foods with a soft texture, which are easy to chew and swallow, make up a soft diet. Tough meats, raw fruits and vegetables, chewy bread products, nuts, and seeds are all things you should avoid eating.

popcorn, potato chips, and other crunchy foods While on a soft diet, you may need to stay away from foods that are high in fiber, cause gas, are greasy, or are spicy. Foods such as vegetables, soups, and fruits can be blended, pureed, steamed, or cooked until they are a consistency that is easier to swallow.

Chapter Two

What Are the Benefits of Soft Foods?

After dental surgery, it's important to eat soft foods to help your body heal properly. Any tooth extraction, periodontal surgery, implants, or surgery on your tooth's root are all examples of oral surgery. If you have oral surgery, you must eat only soft foods and avoid biting with the affected tooth to prevent irritation. Following oral surgery, your mouth and jaw may be sore.

Inability to chew properly is one of the most common reasons for eating soft foods. Hard foods may be difficult to chew for an elderly person with poor dental health. A soft diet may also be recommended if you've had oral surgery, are missing teeth, or have dentures. If you have difficulty swallowing for any reason, a soft diet may be recommended.

Some people lose their ability to swallow properly after a stroke, which can be temporary or permanent.

Choking and aspiration are less likely when you eat easy-to-swallow foods. You may have difficulty swallowing or pain when swallowing after neck surgery. Radiation to the neck, throat, or chest, as well as any type of cancer in these areas, can make it difficult to chew or swallow.

A soft diet will be started as a transitional diet back to normal eating after being sedated and on intravenous nutrition or tube feeding following surgery or an emergency. You'll most likely begin with a clear liquid diet and work your way up to a full liquid or pureed diet. You'll be able to start a soft diet once you've demonstrated that you can swallow and digest these foods without causing any problems. If chewing and swallowing soft foods proves difficult, you may need to temporarily switch to a pureed or liquid diet.

Chapter Three

What's the best way to cook soft foods?

What's the best way to cook soft foods?

Because they are easier to swallow, cut food into small pieces of 12 inch or less in size.

Cook or moisten meats and vegetables using chicken broth, beef broth, gravy, or sauces. Cook until the vegetables are tender enough to mash with a fork.

To make foods easier to chew and swallow, use a food processor to grind or puree them.

To blend the fruits, use fruit juice.

Soups with meat or vegetables larger than 12 inches in length should be strained.

Instructions for use

Eat in a serene, unhurried setting. It's possible that the way you eat is just as important as the food you consume. While eating, don't rush. Take your time chewing and swallowing your food.

Eat small, frequent meals throughout the day, but avoid eating within two hours of going to bed.

Avoid foods that make you feel nauseous.

Do not take aspirin or ibuprofen, which are NSAIDs (nonsteroidal anti-inflammatory drugs). Also avoid medicine that contain aspirin. NSAIDs can cause ulcers and delay or prevent ulcer healing.

Use antacids as needed, but keep in mind that magnesium-containing antacids may cause diarrhea.

Chapter Four

Who Is Appropriate for a Soft-Food Diet?

Who Is Appropriate for a Soft-Food Diet?

Your doctor will let you know if you need to eat this way. It can be helpful in situations like these:

Post Surgery: If you have recently undergone head, neck, or stomach surgery, your doctor will ask you to be on a soft food diet. A few examples of these kinds of surgeries are bariatric surgery and gastrectomy.

After surgery. It's common to follow a soft food diet while you recover from certain operations. Your doctor might recommend it if you've recently had surgery on your:

Chapter Five

Mouth Tooth Head Neck Stomach

Mouth Tooth Head Neck Stomach

Dental Problems: Wisdom tooth extraction and loose dentures are very common. During this time, you must be on a soft food diet so that you do not have to make an effort to chew. The soft texture of foods will allow you to swallow the food directly. This will also prevent the possibility of food getting stuck and infection. A doctor may propose a soft foods-only diet for patients with:

Dental pain A loose tooth

Recent oral or throat surgery or tonsillectomy Recent endoscopy

Difficulty Swallowing: In cases of difficulty in swallowing or dysphagia, doctors recommend consuming soft foods. The soft, liquidy texture of the food will allow you to consume it without putting too much stress on the muscles that aid swallowing.

Cancer Treatment: Radiotherapy and chemotherapy mostly cause inflammation of the digestive tract. This condition is also known as mucositis, and patients are recommended to be on a soft diet during this time. Current radiation treatment for cancer of the head or neck.

They might also tell you to follow the diet if you're getting radiation therapy to your head, neck, or stomach. Issues with digestion. A soft diet helps some people who have digestive

problems. The foods in the diet are easy to digest, so your digestive tract won't have to work as hard to break them down. This type of eating plan also features mild foods that are less likely to irritate your gut.

Chapter Six

What is the purpose of a soft food diet and why is it recommended?

What is the purpose of a soft food diet and why is it recommended?

Soft food diets consist of soft, easily digestible foods and are prescribed to people who can't tolerate normally textured or highly seasoned foods. you might be wondering what this means. A soft food diet refers to food that is soft in texture, low in fiber and easy to digest. This way of eating is sometimes called a gastrointestinal (GI) soft diet. It is used after surgery or gut upset. Eat foods from "easy to digest" list and avoid foods on "difficult to digest list." Follow this diet for as long as your healthcare provider recommends.

This could be the next two to three weeks or until your appetite and bowel movements return to normal. If you have a hard time eating at home, contact your dietitian or physician. If a food upsets your stomach or causes gas, avoid that food for a few days before you try it again. Read food labels on all packaged food. Pick foods that contain less than 2 grams of fiber per serving. Your healthcare provider has prescribed a soft diet.

This means eating foods that are soft, low in fiber, and easy to digest. This diet is for people with digestive problems. This should not be confused with a soft diet that is prescribed for people with issues chewing and swallowing. A soft diet provides foods that are easy to chew and swallow. It will reduce or prevent stomach pain or discomfort. Foods should be bite-sized and very soft or moist.

Follow your healthcare provider's specific instructions about what foods and drinks you may have. The general guidelines below can help you get started on this diet.

Unless your dietitian or healthcare provider gives you different instructions, you can use these guidelines to help you decide which soft foods to eat. If you can't tolerate a food, avoid that food for a few weeks before you try it again. You have been prescribed a soft diet (also called gastrointestinal soft diet or bland diet) (also called gastrointestinal soft diet or bland diet).

This reduces the amount of work your digestive tract has to do. It also reduces the chance that your digestive tract will be irritated by the food you eat. A soft diet is prescribed for people with digestive problems. The diet consists of foods that are tender, mildly seasoned, and easy to digest. While on this diet, you should not eat fried or spicy foods, or raw fruits and vegetables. Also don't drink alcoholic beverages. Healthcare providers commonly prescribed these diets to people with certain medical conditions or who are recovering from surgery.

Soft food diets are used in many settings, including hospitals, long-term care facilities, and in the home. They're typically followed for short periods of a few days to a few weeks, though some circumstances may require the diet to be followed for a longer period. Soft diets are often used to treat swallowing disorders, collectively known as dysphagia. Dysphagia is common in older adults and those with neurological disorders and neurodegenerative diseases.

Although the point of texture-modified diets is to reduce the risk of aspiration and pneumonia in people with dysphagia, current research suggests that modifying food texture may result in a worsened quality of life and undernutrition, highlighting the need for more research.

In addition to dysphagia, soft diets are prescribed to people who have recently undergone mouth or jaw surgery that has affected their ability to chew.

For example, people who have undergone wisdom teeth removal, major jaw surgery, or dental implant surgery may need to follow a soft diet to promote healing.

Soft diets are also used as transitional diets between full liquid or puréed diets and regular diets in people who have undergone abdominal surgery or are recovering from gastrointestinal illness to allow the digestive system to heal more effectively.

Additionally, soft diets can be prescribed to people who are too weak to consume regular foods, such as those undergoing chemotherapy, as well as to people who have lost feeling in their face or mouth or can't control their lips or tongue due to a stroke.

Although soft food diets used in both the clinical and home setting can vary, most that are used in the short term are low in fiber and bland to ease digestibility and the comfort of the person eating the diet. Keep in mind that some people have to be on soft food diets for longer periods. In these cases, the diet may be higher in fiber and more flavorful than soft diets used in the short term.

Chapter Seven

Soft Food Diets: What They Are and What They Aren't

Soft Food Diets: What They Are and What They Aren't

There are two different kinds:

Dietary soft mechanical This includes foods that you don't need to chew as much. You'll eat things with different textures and thicknesses that are chopped, ground, mashed, or puréed. These foods are soft and tender, and you should be able to mash them with a fork.

Puréed soft diet: This is a bit more limited than a mechanical soft diet. You'll only eat foods that you don't need to chew at all. As the name implies, you can eat meals that include puréed foods or liquid foods. Liquids can be added to make swallowing easier.

Foods to eat on a soft food diet

Soft diets are used when regular-textured or highly seasoned foods can't be tolerated, which can happen for a number of reasons. Soft diets should not be confused with puréed diets. Although puréed foods are allowed on soft food diets, puréed diets are entirely different.

Overall, soft diets should consist of foods that are soft, as well as easy to eat and digest. Here are some examples of foods that can be enjoyed on most soft diets:

Fruits & Vegetables: Fruits are an important component of a soft food diet. They add to the nutritional values of your meals with their high contents of fiber, vitamins, and minerals. Most fruits are very juicy and are a great source of energetic water and There is no need to explain how beneficial vegetables are for your health and recovery.

They are filled with vital nutrients and are included in every diet. Cooked, peeled apples or applesauce, bananas, avocado, peeled ripe peaches, cooked pears, puréed fruits, etc. you can try:

Chapter Eight

Chopped cooked spinach Applesauce

Canned fruit

Soft cooked carrots

Steamed or soft-cooked vegetables

Soft, skinless fruits, like bananas, stone fruits, and melons
Baked fruits

Salad greens Green beans

Well-cooked broccoli florets Cooked zucchini without seeds

Ingredients

1 ripe banana

3 tablespoons porridge oats 1 cup low-fat milk

1 drop of vanilla essence

The Best Way To Get Ready

Blitz the oats in a dry blender jar.

Add milk, banana, and vanilla essence.

Blitz well (make sure that there are no banana lumps). Pour into a glass or bottle and drink up.

Most fresh fruits and vegetables are too hard to eat when you are on a soft diet, but there are many other options. Besides ripe bananas, which are soft enough to eat fresh, you should only eat cooked or canned fruits, or applesauce. If you are able to tolerate thin liquids, you can try 100 percent fruit juices or nectar. For vegetables, you should cook all types, except perhaps finely chopped lettuce, until they are soft enough to mash with a fork, or choose soft canned vegetables.

Some good vegetable examples are mashed skinless potatoes, canned green beans and cooked spinach.

To get a variety of fruits and vegetables packed into one serving, try making a smoothie blended very well with various fruits and vegetables, such as bananas, peaches, carrots and juice.

Eggs: They are packed full of proteins and most all the vitamins, except for vitamin C. They are also rich in such minerals as calcium, iron, magnesium, phosphorus, potassium, zinc, selenium, and others. Eggs possess a great number of health benefits as well. They may promote muscle strength, boost your brain processes, add to energy production, strengthen your immune system, improve your skin and eye health, reduce the risk of heart disease and others. cooked whole eggs or egg whites, egg salad, eggs are an excellent source of protein and provide 13 essential nutrients.

These nutrients assist the body during recovery from illness or surgery," Upton says. For a flavor and fat boost, fold in some cheese, Berg recommends.

Dairy products: Dairy products are perfect for this diet, as most of them have a soft texture, or even a liquid form. Most dairy products are extremely rich in calcium and protein, not to mention the great number of such nutrients as magnesium, folate, and vitamins A, B1, B2, B6, B12, D, and E. They offer such health benefits as the improvement of your bone density, boosting muscle building processes, reducing the risk of cancer and improving heart health.

Lower fat dairy products are typically recommended for people recovering from gastrointestinal surgery or illness. Choose dairy products that are high in protein, like:

Chapter Nine

Moistened pancakes and waffles

You should, however, avoid pieces of hard cheeses, like cubes of cheddar or Swiss cheese, and any product that has added nuts, seeds or granola, such as certain varieties of yogurt. Because cheese is relatively high in calories, you can add extra cheese or cheese sauces to your foods if you need to increase your energy intake.

This can be especially helpful if you are underweight or are having difficulty reaching your energy needs due to the restrictions of a soft diet. Milk is another dairy option, but you should check with your doctor first to make sure you are allowed to drink thin liquids, since some people on soft diets have troubling swallowing them.

Grains and starches: Grains are an inseparable part of any well-balanced nutritional plan.

They are one of the main sources of fiber and offer a lot of minerals and vitamins.

These give you carbs, a good source of energy. Choose grains that are low in fiber so that they're easy to digest, like:

Mashed potatoes, sweet potatoes Bread Soft cereals

Hot cereals, like cream of wheat or oatmeal Soft pasta and noodles

White rice

Ingredients

Chapter Ten

The Best Way To Get Ready

Place the potato halves in a large soup pot containing water. Close the lid and let the potato boil and become soft.

Take the potatoes out with a ladle or fork.

Peel the potatoes and toss them into a large bowl. Use a masher to mash the potatoes well.

You can also use the back of the fork to mash the potatoes.

Add in the crème fraîche, pureed cottage cheese, unsalted butter, and salt. Combine well.

You may add finely chopped herbs, but make sure they don't irritate your stomach or make it difficult for you to swallow the food.

Chapter Eleven

Soft-cooked vegetables

Many breads are easy to chew, but some types can be difficult to swallow. Avoid breads and crackers made with whole grains or oats, or those that contain added nuts, seeds or raisins, as these can get caught in your throat or esophagus when you are swallowing.

Some good bread and grain options include soft enriched breads, plain crackers and cooked oatmeal with milk. If you are eating bread, crackers or cereal that is dry, try moistening the food with milk or another liquid to make it easier to swallow.

If you are not supposed to have thin liquids, make sure the food absorbs all of the liquid. Well-cooked rice and pasta are two other grain products you can eat when you are on a soft diet.

Meat, poultry, and fish: Meat is a great source of proteins and is vital for the recovery, and maintenance of all the internal processes. You should eat minced meats cooked in stews and casseroles, and any moist, tender meats or poultry. An excellent choice is fish that is rich in omega-3 fatty and certain nutrients and vitamins, which are also highly important for the healing process and health of your bones and muscle tissues.

Finely chopped or ground moistened poultry, soft tuna or chicken salad (without chopped raw vegetables or fruit like celery or apples), baked or broiled fish, soft meatballs, soft tofu, etc.

Soups: puréed or broth-based soups with soft-cooked vegetables

Miscellaneous: gravies, sauces, smooth nut butters, unseeded jellies and jams.

Ingredients

200 g boneless chicken cubes 1 cup pearl couscous

½ cup button mushrooms, halved 3 cups chicken stock

1 cup vegetable stock

½ cup chopped onion 2 inch ginger, grated

1 teaspoon garlic powder 3 tablespoons fresh cream

1 tablespoon unsalted butter Salt to taste

Chapter Twelve

Vegetables and fruits should be washed and peeled before consumption.

Meat, eggs, tofu, and cottage cheese, for example, should be cut into small pieces. Vegetables, meat, fish, lentils, and beans should all be soft before serving.

Using a blender, puree the foods.

In a sieve, strain the soup vegetables.

Keep mashed potatoes, vegetables, and fruits free of lumps. Using butter or crème fraîche, make an egg scramble.

Add milk, cream, or melted cheese to sauces to make them. Make your food more moist by adding stock.

Soup or milk should be used to moisten bread.

What other tips do you have for sticking to a soft food diet?

To achieve a mashed potato consistency, chew all foods slowly. It will be easier for your body to digest your food if you chew it thoroughly.

Throughout the day, keep eating every few hours. Instead of three large meals per day, you might prefer to eat four to six smaller meals each day.

Every day, you should consume at least eight cups of fluid. Pudding, ice cream, sherbet, Popsicles®, soup, gelatin, and yogurt should all be included in your fluid intake.

Due to the restricted foods, this diet may be deficient in certain nutrients. If you're on this diet for more than 2 to 3 weeks, you might need a multivitamin. Before taking any vitamin or mineral supplements, consult with your healthcare provider.

Fiber remains an essential component of a healthy diet. Slowly reintroduce fiber-rich foods into your diet once your symptoms have subsided. To avoid stomach upset, introduce one new food into your diet every 2–3 days.

It is essential for good health to consume a diverse diet. A sample one-day menu is provided below, which should be easy to tolerate during the first two to three weeks following surgery.

Recipes and snacks for a soft food diet

It can be difficult to stick to a restrictive diet, especially when many healthy foods, such as raw fruits and vegetables, are forbidden. Those on soft diets, however, have a wide variety of tasty meal and snack options.

Here are some suggestions for soft-diet meals:

Inspiration for breakfast

avocado slices and scrambled eggs

cooked peaches and creamy cashew butter on top of cream of wheat

Eggs, goat cheese, spinach, and butternut squash are used in this crustless quiche.

yogurt parfait made with unsweetened yogurt, banana or canned peaches, seedless blueberry jam, and smooth almond butter.

Chapter Thirteen

Caution with Mouth Pain

It's important that all meals and snacks be as balanced as possible and include high protein foods, especially for those who have recently undergone surgery or have higher nutrient needs, such as those with cancer

Easy-to-follow guidelines for those on a soft-drink diet

Although consuming a diet consisting of only soft foods can be difficult, the following tips may make following such a diet easier:

Choose healthy options: While soft, sugar-laden foods like cakes and pastries may seem appealing, ensuring you're consuming healthy foods like vegetables, fruits, and proteins is best for your health. Choose a variety of nutrient-rich foods.

Season your food: Using herbs and other mild seasonings can help make food more palatable.

Focus on protein: Adding protein to every meal and snack is especially important for people recovering from surgery and those who are malnourished.

Eat small, consistent meals: Rather than consuming large meals, it's recommended to consume multiple small meals throughout the day when following a soft diet.

Eat slowly and chew thoroughly: Taking your time while eating and chewing food thoroughly is important for many people on soft diets, including those recovering from abdominal surgery and with neurological conditions. Sit upright and take small sips of liquid between bites.

Plan meals ahead of time: Finding meals that work with a mechanical soft diet can be difficult. Planning meals ahead of time can help reduce stress and make mealtime easier.

Keep appliances handy: Blenders, strainers, and food processors can be used to create delicious, soft-diet-approved recipes.

Typically, soft diets are used as transitional diets for short periods until a person is ready to start eating a regular-consistency diet again. Your healthcare provider will give you instructions on how long you should follow a soft food diet, while a registered dietitian can provide you with any other pertinent information.

What Are the Benefits of Eating Soft Foods?

A soft foods diet or no chew diet can help make it easier to eat when chewing hurts. Most people will follow a soft food diet temporarily.

Those without teeth (or dentures) may be following a soft foods diet long term. Let's look at some of the reasons to follow a soft foods diet.

Soft Foods for Mouth Pain. You may be looking to follow a soft foods diet if you have mouth pain.

Mouth pain may be caused by dental issues. Untreated cavities or gingivitis can make it difficult to eat. When you bite down you experience significant pain.

The solution is to find foods that do no require chewing. So, you don't have to bite down.

Rather, you can mush food around in your mouth before a swallow.

After a dental procedure, it's best to stick to soft foods.

Having mouth or dental surgery can cause temporary pain requiring a soft foods diet. Having wisdom teeth removed, oral surgery, or even just getting tight braces placed can cause temporary mouth pain making it difficult to chew.

A soft foods diet can help you get through the first days and weeks following dental surgery (or any type of dental procedure) (or any type of dental procedure). Over time, as the pain goes away you can transition back to a normal diet.

If you are looking for soft foods to eat because chewing hurts, it is so important to address the underlying issues causing your pain.

While dental or oral health care is expensive, if left untreated it can lead to significant health issues.

Chewing should not hurt. Pain is your body's way of saying something is wrong.

It is important to find the underlying issue causing your mouth pain. Treating the mouth pain can mean you go back to following a regular diet sooner.

And while rare, mouth pain can be a sign of oral cancer. Additionally, untreated cavities or mouth sores can lead to an infection or heart issues.

Be sure to work with your healthcare team to resolve any ongoing issues you have with mouth pain.

Tips for Selecting Soft Foods to Eat

Let's talk about tips for selecting soft foods to eat.

Every person is in a different situation. Maybe you need every food you eat to be smooth or pureed. But maybe you can manage some texture as long as it's soft.

The key making foods easier to eat when chewing hurts is: soft, tender, moist foods.

Tender and Moist

Making sure foods are tender is important when following a soft foods diet.

If you are eating grains, make sure you cook them extra long so they are soft and mushy.

When cooking meat, cook them low and slow (crock pots work great) until the meat falls apart with a fork. Adding extra moisture and/or cutting the meat can help make it even easier to eat.

Adding more liquid during the cooking process and/or to foods when serving can make them easier to eat. Think of adding gravy to mashed potatoes. Or a splash of cream to oatmeal. If a food is too dry, even if it is soft, it can be difficult to eat.

Premade Soft Foods

You can make foods soft by blending them, mushing them, cooking them slow, and/or adding liquid.

Or you can select foods that are already soft.

Canned foods are a great example of premade soft foods. The process of canning requires heat and liquid. This makes the canned food quite soft and easy to eat. Not all canned foods are soft and easy to eat. For example, canned pineapple can be a little difficult due to the texture of pineapple. But canned mandarin oranges or diced peaches can be quite soft and easy to eat.

Remember, everyone tolerates softs foods differently. This is based on their individual situation. The soft foods to eat below are ideas to get you started. Over time you will find your favorite soft foods that make eating less painful.

When chewing hurts, eat soft foods.

Here is our list of foods to eat when chewing hurts. This list doesn't include every single soft foods ever created. It's just some ideas to get you started. The foods are listed in alphabetical order (no special ranking for the "best" since everyone tolerates foods differently). I hope this list provides you with some inspiration for soft food you can eat and also note some have been mentioned ealier in this guide, listed again for more clarifications

Almond butter Applesauce Avocados Banana (ripe) (ripe)

Bean dip (smooth) (smooth) Beans (well-cooked) (well-cooked) Beef stew (well cooked) (well cooked) Brie (w/o skin)

Broccoli cheddar soup

Broth (beef, chicken, vegetable) (beef, chicken, vegetable) Carrots (canned) (canned)

Cheese spread Cheesecake

Chicken noodle soup Cottage Cheese

Cheese (Cream Cheese) (Cream Cheese) Cream of mushroom soup Cream of Wheat Creamed spinach

Custard Egg salad Flan

Frozen yogurt

Fruit cocktail (canned) (canned) Fudge bars

Green beans (canned) (canned) Grits

Guacamole

Hard boiled eggs Hummus

Ice-cream Jam\sJell-O Juice Kefir

Lentil soup Lentils

Macaroni and cheese Mandarin oranges (canned) (canned) Mashed cauliflower\sMashed potatoes (regular or sweet) (regular or sweet) Meat loaf

Milk Mousse

Nutrition drinks Oatmeal (well cooked) (well cooked) Pancakes

Pasta\sPeaches (canned) (canned) Peanut butter Pears (canned) (canned) Poached eggs Polenta Popsicles

Potato soup Protein shakes Pudding

Rice (well cooked & moist) (well cooked & moist) Salmon

Scrambled eggs Shakes

Sherbet

Shredded beef (tender & moist) (tender & moist) Shredded chicken (tender & moist) (tender & moist) Sloppy Joes

Smoothies Soft bread Sorbet Soufflé tapioca Tilapia Tofu (soft) (soft)

Tomato soup Tuna\syogurt (smooth) (smooth)

Meal Plan Without Chewing

Now we covered a lot of different soft foods to eat. But what does that look like in a meal or throughout the day. Here is another example of a soft foods or no chew meal plan for a day.

Breakfast soft foods

From eggs to soft cooked grains to yogurt and smoothies. Breakfast is an easy meal to incorporate soft foods to eat. In fact, many of these foods you may already eat for breakfast.

Breakfast With Soft Foods:

Chapter Fourteen

Beef and vegetable stew Applesauce Iced tea

Beef and vegetable stew Applesauce Iced tea

Soft Foods Dinner

Finding soft foods to eat for dinner is often the most challenging meal. Here is a delicious soft foods dinner idea.

Dinner with Soft Samples:

Meat loaf with gravy Mashed potatoes with gravy Canned green beans

Soft Foods Snacks

In addition to 3 solid meals, you may be looking for some food soft foods snack ideas. Here is a list of some tasty soft foods snacks.

Snacks Made with Soft Food:

Yogurt topped with jam

Cottage cheese with canned peaches Egg salad

High Calorie Smoothies

Wait until you're told to eat the following items.

Steer clear of these until you're feeling better. These foods are harder to chew, have high fiber content, and are difficult to digest.

Slowly Returning to Crunchy Foods

Carbonated drinks (soda and seltzer) spicy foods

jams/jellies with seeds

whole spices such as peppercorns

Recipes for moist food

Any diet can feel restrictive at first, but there are a bunch of delicious ways to prepare soft foods. Here are a few to try:

**

Green goddess smoothie Creamy tomato soup Vegan mashed potatoes Banana pudding

Make sure everything is in order.

Here are some tips to make your food as soft and gentle on your gut as possible:

Grind, purée, or cut food into small pieces.

Mash foods, including veggies, fruits, and potatoes. Use sauces like gravy or broth to moisten foods further.

Increase the amount of nutrients you consume

You might not feel as hungry as usual when you're in recovery, but you need nutrients more than ever. Incorporate nutrient-rich fortified drinks like Ensure or Boost, which are formulated to fill that nutrition gap when you're not eating enough due to loss of appetite or dietary restrictions. If you're losing weight due to treatments or loss of appetite, opt for higher fat foods to help increase your calorie intake. (Like you needed an excuse to eat more avocados.) Be sure to let your doctor know if you're experiencing unexpected weight loss.

Your surgeon or dentist will tell you when it's okay to start trying crunchy or hard foods like chips, cereals, or crunchy vegetables. You can ask your dentist care professional for more specific instructions. It varies by the case of how long your dentist or oral surgeon may advise sticking to a soft food diet. Follow your aftercare instructions to keep your mouth healthy during the healing process and beyond.

Soft Food Diet Explained

Dieters are recommended to introduce plenty of variety to make sure you receive all kinds of nutrition while you eat only soft foods. Try to construct your diet menu around the below- mentioned food options:

Chapter Seventeen

Carbs

Carbonated drinks (soda and seltzer) spicy foods

jams/jellies with seeds

whole spices such as peppercorns

Recipes for moist food

Any diet can feel restrictive at first, but there are a bunch of delicious ways to prepare soft foods. Here are a few to try:

**

Green goddess smoothie Creamy tomato soup Vegan mashed potatoes Banana pudding

Make sure everything is in order.

Here are some tips to make your food as soft and gentle on your gut as possible:

Grind, purée, or cut food into small pieces.

Mash foods, including veggies, fruits, and potatoes. Use sauces like gravy or broth to moisten foods further.

Increase the amount of nutrients you consume

You might not feel as hungry as usual when you're in recovery, but you need nutrients more than ever. Incorporate nutrient-rich fortified drinks like Ensure or Boost, which are formulated to fill that nutrition gap when you're not eating enough due to loss of appetite or dietary restrictions. If you're losing weight due to treatments or loss of appetite, opt for higher fat foods to help increase your calorie intake. (Like you needed an excuse to eat more avocados.) Be sure to let your doctor know if you're experiencing unexpected weight loss.

Slowly Returning to Crunchy Foods

Your surgeon or dentist will tell you when it's okay to start trying crunchy or hard foods like chips, cereals, or crunchy vegetables. You can ask your dentist care professional for more specific instructions. It varies by the case of how long your dentist or oral surgeon may advise sticking to a soft food diet. Follow your aftercare instructions to keep your mouth healthy during the healing process and beyond.

Soft Food Diet Explained

Dieters are recommended to introduce plenty of variety to make sure you receive all kinds of nutrition while you eat only soft foods. Try to construct your diet menu around the below- mentioned food options:

Chapter Eighteen

Optional desserts

Milky pudding made from tapioca, semolina or rice Egg custard or crème caramel

Fruit mousse Greek yogurt

Mashed fruit along ice cream, evaporated milk or custard Homemade trifle

Butter and bread pudding Fruit sorbet

How Long Should You Eat Soft Foods?

You will be on a soft food diet as per your doctor's recommendation. It is best to avoid eating anything solid that might aggravate the pain or inflammation. Yes, being on a soft food diet will be a tad boring, but you must design your meals in a way that there's sufficient gap between two meals, and the foods that you consume are tasty.

Conclusion

A soft food diet is typically recommended short-term to give your digestive system a break after certain medical procedures. It consists of mushy low-fiber foods. Cooked fruits and vegetables, easily chewable proteins, and soft starches can be enjoyed when following a soft food diet. Foods that are difficult to chew and digest, as well as spicy and acidic foods, should typically be avoided when following a soft food diet.

It's possible to consume healthy and tasty meals and snacks when following a soft diet. Meals and snacks should be nutrient-rich to promote healing and overall health. Choosing nutritious foods, focusing on protein, planning ahead, eating small meals frequently, and taking your time while eating are all smart tips for people following soft food diets.

According to the University of Michigan, eating a balanced diet of enough calories and plenty of protein can help you heal. Protein helps build and repair muscle, skin, and tissue.

You can easily get lots of protein from protein powder mixed with milk or water. Or you can soup with beef or chicken broth can add more grams of protein to your meal. There are several soft fruit and veggie options to ensure you get adequate nutrition while healing. For example, you can eat mashed avocado to get the small amount of recommended healthy fat you need per day. Peaches, kiwi, and strawberries are soft and high in vitamin C, which helps repair tissues.

Healthcare providers commonly prescribe soft food diets to help people recover from surgery and illness and make chewing and digesting food easier.

When following a soft food diet, it's important to choose soft, easily digestible foods and avoid foods that are hard to chew or digest. Spicy and potentially irritating foods should likewise be avoided. Although a soft food diet can be difficult to follow, it's used to promote recovery, so it's important to follow your healthcare provider's instructions and comply until you're ready to transition back to a regular diet.

When it comes to recovering from surgery, reducing inflammation of the stomach or GI tract, and dealing with the pain due to wisdom tooth extraction or loose dentures, a soft food diet is the best. It will help you get all the nutrients and accelerate your recovery. Make sure to go on this diet only if your doctor advises you to. Get well soon. A soft diet can get boring if you stick to the basic foods such as soups, jelly and eggs. But you can still eat many of your favourite foods. Try to be creative and find ways to soften them. A liquidiser works well for many foods. But foods like bread and fish with bones are less suitable to liquidise. You may feel too tired to cook if you are having treatment for cancer. Buy ready meals at your supermarket if you don't have someone to cook for you. You can also liquidise theseif necessary.

Chapter Nineteen

Conclusion

Choices for the Main Course

CPSIA information can be obtained
at www.ICGtesting.com
Printed in the USA
LVHW050815010422
714993LV00007B/259

9 781804 383704